**MILITARY TECHNOLOGIES**

# TECHNOLOGY DURING THE CIVIL WAR

JOANNE MATTERN

**Checkerboard Library**

An Imprint of Abdo Publishing
abdopublishing.com

# ABDOPUBLISHING.COM

Published by Abdo Publishing, a division of ABDO, PO Box 398166, Minneapolis, Minnesota 55439. Copyright © 2017 by Abdo Consulting Group, Inc. International copyrights reserved in all countries. No part of this book may be reproduced in any form without written permission from the publisher. Checkerboard Library™ is a trademark and logo of Abdo Publishing.

Printed in the United States of America, North Mankato, Minnesota
102016
012017

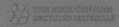
THIS BOOK CONTAINS
RECYCLED MATERIALS

Content Developer: Nancy Tuminelly
Design and Production: Mighty Media, Inc.
Series Editor: Rebecca Felix
Cover Photo: Library of Congress
Interior Photos: Alamy, p. 21; AP Images, pp. 6, 24; Getty Images, p. 13; iStockphoto, p. 17; Library of Congress, pp. 5, 14, 19; Records of the National Archives and Records Administration, Record Group 64, p. 23; Shutterstock Images, p. 8; Wikimedia Commons, pp. 9 (left, right), 11, 27, 29

## Publisher's Cataloging-in-Publication Data

Names: Mattern, Joanne, author.
Title: Technology during the Civil War / by Joanne Mattern.
Description: Minneapolis, MN : Abdo Publishing, 2017. | Series: Military
     technologies | Includes bibliographical references and index.
Identifiers: LCCN 2016944835 | ISBN 9781680784114 (lib. bdg.) |
     ISBN 9781680797640 (ebook)
Subjects:  LCSH:  United States--History--Civil War, 1861-1865--Technology--
     Juvenile literature. | Technology--United States--History--19th century--
     Juvenile literature.
Classification: DDC 973.7/8--dc23
LC record available at http://lccn.loc.gov/2016944835

# CONTENTS

# AMERICA DIVIDED

In the mid-1800s, the United States of America became a nation divided by war. North and South fought one another in bloody battles over four years. This conflict was caused by great differences between Northern and Southern states.

The North had a larger population and more cities than the South. Many of these cities were the sites of manufacturing centers and factories. The economy in this part of the country was industrial.

The economy in the South was based on farming. The most important crops were tobacco and cotton, which were grown on plantations. Southern plantation owners relied on slaves to plant and harvest these crops.

Many in the South believed their economy would fall apart without slave labor. For this reason, many Southerners were upset with abolitionists. Abolitionists were people who supported the end of slavery.

Slavery was in practice across America for hundreds of years. By 1804, Northern states had abolished slavery.

The Northern states were free. They were home to many abolitionists. One was Abraham Lincoln, who was elected president in 1860. Lincoln did not have the support of Southern states. Many Southerners feared Lincoln becoming president would mean the end of slavery in their states.

Because of this fear, South Carolina voted to **secede** from the United States on December 20, 1860.

Mississippi, Florida, Alabama, Georgia, Louisiana, and Texas followed. In February 1861, these seven states formed a new nation. It was called the Confederate States of America, or the Confederacy. The states that didn't **secede** were called the Union.

The Confederacy soon began taking over federal military forts in the South.  On April 12, 1861, a brief battle broke out between Union and Confederate troops at Fort Sumter, South Carolina.

Lincoln viewed this battle as an act of war.  In response, he prepared troops to invade the South.  Meanwhile, the Southern states of Virginia, Tennessee, Arkansas, and North Carolina joined the Confederacy.  The Civil War had begun.

The Civil War lasted four years.  The South fought for independence.  The North fought to preserve the United States.  Later, its aim was also to abolish slavery.  Lincoln signed the **Emancipation** Proclamation in September 1862.  It went into effect in January 1863.

The Civil War is often referred to as the first modern war.  This was due to the many **technological** advancements at the time.  **Firearms** were more **accurate** and could fire more **rounds**.  Cannons and howitzers became more advanced and deadlier.  The Civil War would change how soldiers in future wars fought and the weapons they used.

# TIMELINE

**DECEMBER 20, 1860**

South Carolina becomes the first state to **secede** from the Union.

**APRIL 12, 1861**

War begins when Confederate soldiers attack Union troops at Fort Sumter.

**SEPTEMBER 22, 1862**

Abraham Lincoln signs the **Emancipation** Proclamation. It will go into effect on January 1, 1863.

**FEBRUARY 1861**

The Confederate States of America is formed.

**SEPTEMBER 17, 1862**

Union forces defeat Robert E. Lee's army at the Battle of Antietam.

**SEPTEMBER 2, 1864**

The Union army captures Atlanta, Georgia. It is one of the South's most important cities.

**APRIL 9, 1865**

Lee surrenders, leading to the end of the war.

**JULY 3, 1863**

Lee's army is defeated during the Battle of Gettysburg.

**APRIL 2, 1865**

Union forces capture Richmond, Virginia, the capital of the Confederacy.

# ⊰②⊱ EDGED WEAPONS

**Civil War soldiers faced off in close combat on the battlefield.** They used small arms during these attacks. These included edged weapons such as swords, sabers, bayonets, and knives. These weapons were not only useful in battle, but also for survival as troops traveled.

Swords were sharp and deadly weapons. But they were not often used as weapons in the Civil War. Instead, they were carried by officers as symbols of their rank.

**Cavalry** riders carried sabers for similar reasons, especially in Union armies. Sabers were similar to swords. But they had a curved blade instead of a straight one.

Knives were the most resourceful edged weapon of the Civil War. The most popular was the bowie knife, which was used by both Union and Confederate soldiers. This knife had a large blade that was useful in combat.

But bowie knives were more useful when soldiers were not fighting. Most used them while they were in camp.

A bowie knife was very handy to open a can or cut down a small tree!

The edged weapons most used in battle by both Northern and Southern soldiers were bayonets. These were long blades that could be attached to the ends of certain muskets or rifles. The soldiers could shoot at their enemy with the **firearm** from a distance. They could also pierce them with the bayonet at close range.

**11**

# FIREARMS

**F**irearms **were essential weapons in Civil War ground battles.** Improvements were made to these small weapons during the war. They became more **accurate** and easier to load.

Rifled muskets were a common type of Civil War firearm. Loading these weapons required many steps. The longer it took soldiers to complete this process in battle, the longer they were exposed to enemy fire. So, soldiers practiced loading their rifles over and over before they went into battle.

In addition to being difficult to load, early muskets were not very accurate. They were smoothbore weapons. This meant the inside of the barrel that the bullet shot through was polished smooth. It could not affect the movement of the bullet.

Long before the Civil War, gun makers had discovered that adding a groove inside of the barrel made the bullet

spin as it was fired. This spinning helped the bullet travel with greater **accuracy**. Muskets that had grooved barrels were called rifled muskets.

However, rifled muskets were still difficult to load. To use the groove, bullets needed to be close to the exact width of the barrel. This tight fit was troublesome when soldiers needed to reload in a hurry. Minié (MIH-nee) balls resolved this problem.

Minié balls were small bullets invented in France in years before the war.  These small bullets fit easily into a rifle's barrel, making them quick to load.  When the rifle was fired, the powder inside its barrel exploded.  Minié balls were designed to expand from the resulting pressure.  This pushed out their sides so they caught the barrel's grooves.

During combat, **cavalry** soldiers of the Civil War preferred rifles with shorter barrels.  These were easier to carry and use on horseback.  Later in the war, the most popular short-barreled rifle in the Union army was the Spencer repeating carbine.  This **firearm** could be loaded quickly and held up to seven bullets at a time.

Union soldiers guard a picket station.  This was a location near a battlefield or camp where soldiers were positioned to watch for the enemy advancing.

Soldiers who fought on horseback also used small handguns that were light and quick to load. Like the Spencer repeating carbine, these weapons held several **rounds** at once. Union soldiers used a Colt Army Model 1860 revolver. This handgun could fire six shots without being reloaded. Southerners used a LeMat revolver, which could fire nine shots.

## BATTLE OF GETTYSBURG

In the early days of the Civil War, soldiers on foot marched in lines across the battlefield. When the soldiers used smoothbore muskets that were not very **accurate**, this formation was less deadly. An inaccurate shot would pass harmlessly between the lines of soldiers. However, as rifled muskets replaced smoothbore muskets, the long lines of soldiers became easier targets.

The Union used this effect on July 3, 1863, during the Battle of Gettysburg in Pennsylvania. During battle, the Confederate soldiers charged forward. But Northern soldiers were able to hold their position. They shot the Confederates down with their **artillery** and rifled muskets. The attack was called Pickett's Charge after George Pickett, a Confederate major general that helped lead the charge.

# RAPID-FIRE GUNS

**H**andguns and rifles weren't the only weapons that could fire **round** after round at the enemy. For the first time in battle, rapid-fire guns were introduced. These guns could fire many bullets, one immediately after the other. This made them a terrifying addition to combat.

The Gatling gun was a rapid-fire gun invented early in the war. Inventor Richard Gatling designed it in 1861 and 1862. He sold it to both Union and Confederate armies.

This massive gun was mounted on wheels. It had six barrels. To fire a Gatling gun, a soldier turned a handle. The barrels rotated, each firing several bullets.

In total these guns could fire 350 bullets per minute. However, they frequently jammed. Because of this,

## TECH FACT

In the years following the Civil War, Gatling guns received many improvements. Later models could fire 400 bullets per minute!

the Gatling gun's use during the war was not widespread.

Northern soldiers used another type of **artillery** called the Agar gun. This gun fired about 100 **rounds** per minute. It was similar to the Gatling gun in size. It was also **unreliable** like the Gatling gun. The Agar often misfired. So, it too did not see widespread use during the war.

Gatling created his weapon to be very destructive. He hoped this would discourage armies from taking part in large battles that led to many deaths.

# THE BIG GUNS

**Gatling guns and Agar guns were deadly when functioning properly.** But it was even bigger **artillery** that effectively destroyed forts and killed many men at once. Cannons, howitzers, and mortars were the big guns used by Confederate and Union armies.

Cannons used during the war were so large that they could not be carried even by several men. Instead, they were mounted on stands or wheeled platforms. Six or seven soldiers worked as a team to operate just one of these weapons.

One of the big guns used during the war was the Napoleon cannon. It was thought to be a safe and **reliable** weapon.

## TECH FACT

Cannons were named by the weight of the balls they fired. So, a thirty-two-pound cannon did not weigh 32 pounds (14.5 kg) itself. It shot balls that were this weight.

A row of massive Union mortars sit ready to fire at Confederate troops during the 1862 Battle of Yorktown.

It was also a powerful killing machine, especially at close range.

Howitzers were larger cannons with shorter barrels. Although howitzers could not shoot as far as cannons, they could fire shells high into the air. Mortars had very short barrels and also fired large shells high into the air. Armies often used these types of **artillery** to fire shells over the walls of a fort.

# NAPOLEON CANNON

The Napoleon was a twelve-pound (5.4 kg) smoothbore cannon. It originally came from France, and was named after former French emperor Louis-Napoléon Bonaparte. This big gun was operated by a team of soldiers.

## LOADING

**1.** First, soldiers moved the gun into position. Then a soldier placed his thumb over the firing vent so the gun would not go off early.

**2.** Another soldier placed a **charge** into the muzzle of the gun.

**3.** A soldier poured **ammunition** down the muzzle of the gun. Then, another soldier used a ramrod to push it down into the barrel. The cannon was ready to fire.

## FIRING

**4.** A soldier placed a firing pin into the firing vent. Another soldier then placed a **friction primer** into the vent. The friction primer had a string attached to it.

**5.** When the time was right, yet another soldier yelled "Fire!" This prompted one soldier to pull the string on the primer, creating a spark.

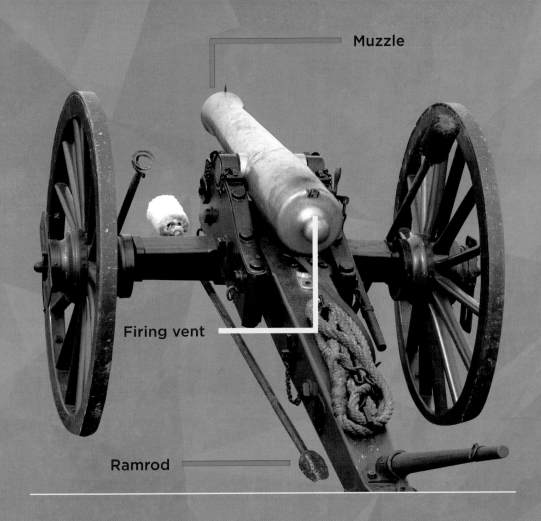

Muzzle

Firing vent

Ramrod

**6.** The spark lit **gunpowder** inside the **friction primer**, causing an explosion. The force of the explosion sent the **ammunition** shooting out of the gun with a loud bang.

**7.** The gun was cleaned out with a ramrod wrapped in cloth. Soon, it was ready to be loaded and fired again.

# ⊱(6)⊰
# THE WAR AT SEA

**T**he massive **artillery** of the Civil War was often **mounted on ships.** This turned these seacraft into giant weapons. Artillery could pierce the hull of a ship and sink it in minutes.

To fight back, warships needed better protection. The solution was to cover them with huge iron plates. Some ships were even built entirely of iron.

These supertough vessels were known as ironclads. They could take multiple hits from enemy fire without suffering much damage. Then, the ironclad would launch its own attack, firing from cannons that were mounted onboard.

Ironclads were the stars of both the Union and Confederate navies. The Union used them to help **blockade** Southern ports and harbors. This prevented supplies getting through to Confederate troops. Some ships made it through. But the blockade successfully

Union ironclad USS *Monitor* and Confederate ironclad CSS *Virginia* launch artillery at one another in Hampton Roads, Virginia.

**crippled** many Confederate armies waiting for supplies.

The Civil War also saw the first successful attack by a submarine. On February 17, 1864, Confederate submarine *Hunley* sank the USS *Housatonic* using a **torpedo**. However, the *Hunley* also sank, killing all of its crew. Despite these losses, this historic battle was an important moment in submarine **warfare**.

The sunken Confederate submarine *Hunley* was raised from the depths of the Atlantic Ocean in 2012. Today, it is on display in Charleston, South Carolina.

One of the new sea weapons used by the navies of the Civil War were underwater mines. These were bombs that exploded under the water. Navies would drop the mines into the water. The mines would sink or float, depending on the type of mine. Then they

# BATTLE OF HAMPTON ROADS

The first battle between armored warships occurred on March 9, 1862. The USS *Monitor* and the CSS *Virginia* fought in the natural harbor of Hampton Roads, Virginia. The day before the fight, the *Virginia* first took on several wooden Union ships. It rammed or fired shells into those ships, sinking them.

The Confederates were sure the *Virginia* could defeat any ship in the Union **fleet**. Then the Confederate navy got a surprise. The Union had an ironclad too! The *Monitor* was small, which made it almost impossible to hit. Its armor was so thick that Confederate shells bounced off! Meanwhile, the *Monitor*'s powerful guns hit the *Virginia* more than 50 times.

By the end of the battle, the two ironclads were still floating, but their crews were exhausted. Both ships retreated to safety. Neither side won this battle. But it became clear to both navies that ironclad ships were the wave of the future.

## IRONCLADS ON THE BATTLEFIELD

would explode when a ship made contact with them. This often caused the ship to sink.

Both the Union and the Confederacy laid mines in the rivers and harbors. The Confederate navy was especially successful using these sea weapons. By the end of the war, it had used mines to destroy dozens of Union ships.

# ≡(7)≡

# BALLOON BATTLES

**C**ivil War battles were not limited to land and sea. Fighting also took to the skies for the first time in US history!  Airplanes had not been invented yet.  But hot-air balloons became the newest **technology** in the war.

Early in the war, balloons were used a few times to observe enemy troops.  The soldiers in the balloons were called aeronauts.  The aeronauts used signal flags to communicate with troops on the ground.  But these flags were hard to see.  So, successfully sending information from the air was difficult.

In 1861, an inventor named Thaddeus Lowe solved this problem.  The **telegraph** had recently been invented. Lowe put a telegraph machine in a balloon named the *Enterprise*.  The telegraph could effectively send messages to troops below.

In June 1861, the *Enterprise* took part in its first military mission.  The Union believed a large Confederate army

was nearby and planning to attack Washington, DC. Lowe went up in the *Enterprise*. He was able to tell the troops that there was no army advancing.

Soon afterward, the Union created the first official Balloon **Corps**. The balloons were then used to scout and spy on the enemy during several famous battles. These include the Battle of Fredericksburg and the Battle of Chancellorsville.

# THE END OF THE WAR

**O**n September 2, 1864, the Union won a major victory when it captured Atlanta, Georgia. This was one of the South's most important cities. The Union captured the Confederate capital of Richmond, Virginia, in April 1865.

The South also claimed several victories during the war. But it could not beat the North in the long run. The North produced weapons and supplies at a rate the South could not match. It also had a better railroad system. This made it easier to get supplies to soldiers on the battlefield.

On April 9, 1865, Confederate General Robert E. Lee surrendered. Southerners knew their loss meant a new way of life. Slavery would soon be abolished across the country, changing the South's economy. And the South's war-damaged cities would need to be rebuilt.

Many Southerners and Confederate supporters were angry over this loss. On April 14, President Lincoln was **assassinated** by a Confederate supporter. His death was

Confederate General Lee surrendered to Union General Ulysses S. Grant at Appomattox Court House, Virginia.

one of about 750,000 in relation to the Civil War.

The Civil War was the bloodiest war ever fought by the United States. It introduced many new **technologies**. **Infantry** weapons were made to be more **accurate**. Ironclads became powerful weapons at sea. And aircraft improvements were useful to military intelligence. The Civil War was the birth of a new age of military technology and **warfare**.

# GLOSSARY

**accurate** — free from error. The state or quality of being free from error is accuracy.

**ammunition** — bullets, shells, cartridges, or other items used in firearms and artillery.

**artillery** — large guns that can be used to shoot over a great distance.

**assassinate** — to murder a very important person, usually for political reasons.

**blockade** — to cut off an area with soldiers or ships. A blockade prevents supplies and people from going into or out of an area.

**cavalry** — a part of an army that fights on horseback.

**charge** — the amount of an explosive material used in a single blast.

**corps** — a group of soldiers that has a certain function.

**cripple** — to cause something or someone to work less efficiently.

**emancipation** — freedom from someone else's control or power.

**essential** — very important or necessary.

**firearm** — a weapon that discharges shots projected by gunpowder.

**fleet** — a group of ships or airplanes under one command.

**friction primer** — a device used to light the explosive in a cannon.

**gunpowder** — a dry explosive substance that is used in firearms.

**infantry** — soldiers trained and organized to fight on foot.

**reliable** — able to be trusted to do or provide what is needed.

**round** — a bullet, shell, or cartridge used for a single shot.

**secede** — to formally break away from a group.

**technology** (tehk-NAH-luh-jee) — machinery and equipment developed for practical purposes using scientific principles and engineering.

**telegraph** — a device that uses electricity to send coded messages over wires.

**torpedo** — a submerged explosive.

**warfare** — methods and weapons used to fight a war.

## WEBSITES

To learn more about **Military Technologies**, visit **booklinks.abdopublishing.com**. These links are routinely monitored and updated to provide the most current information available.

# INDEX